Skimper-Scamper

story by Jeff Newell
illustrations by Barbara Hranilovich

HARCOURT BRACE & COMPANY

Orlando   Atlanta   Austin   Boston   San Francisco   Chicago   Dallas   New York
Toronto   London

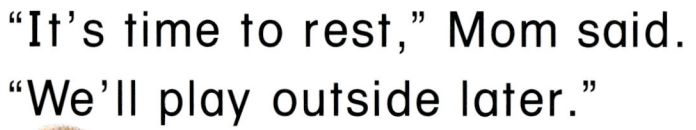

"It's time to rest," Mom said.
"We'll play outside later."

Lisa got her crayons and made a small, blue mouse.

Then—**skimper-scamper**—the mouse ran off the paper!
The mouse grabbed Lisa's jump rope.

"Stop!" said Lisa.
"You're making a mess."

Then Lisa took a yellow crayon and made a cat.
"Get that mouse out of here," she said.

Then—**skimper-scamper**—the cat ran off the paper!

The cat and the mouse had fun with Lisa's paints.

"Oh, no!" said Lisa.
"You're making a big mess."

Quickly Lisa took a black crayon and made a dog.

"Get that cat out of here," she said.

10

Then—**skimper-scamper**—the dog ran off the paper!

The dog, the cat, and the mouse had fun playing ball.

"**Yikes!**" said Lisa.
"You're making a bigger mess.
And Mom's coming back!" Lisa yelled.
"If you help clean up this mess,
I'll give you a ride in my plane."

As Lisa made an airplane,
the animals worked.

Lisa's mom knocked on the door.
"Are you ready to go outside?"
"Just a minute, Mom," said Lisa.

16